SALINE DISTRICT LIBRARY

W9-BAH-306

JE915.96   Yip
Yip, Dora.
Welcome to Cambodia

WITHDRAWN

WELCOME TO MY COUNTRY

Welcome to
CAMBODIA

SALINE DISTRICT LIBRARY
555 N. Maple Road
Saline, MI 48176

Gareth Stevens Publishing
A WORLD ALMANAC EDUCATION GROUP COMPANY

Written by
DORA YIP/DAYANEETHA DE SILVA

Edited in USA by
DOROTHY L. GIBBS

Designed by
JAILANI BASARI

Picture research by
SUSAN JANE MANUEL

First published in North America in 2001 by
Gareth Stevens Publishing
A World Almanac Education Group Company
330 West Olive Street, Suite 100
Milwaukee, Wisconsin 53212 USA

Please visit our web site at:
www.garethstevens.com
For a free color catalog describing
Gareth Stevens' list of high-quality books
and multimedia programs, call
1-800-542-2595 (USA) or
1-800-461-9120 (CANADA).
Gareth Stevens Publishing's
Fax: (414) 332-3567.

All rights reserved. No parts of this book may be reproduced or
utilized in any form or by any means electronic or mechanical,
including photocopying, recording, or by an information storage and
retrieval system, without permission from the copyright owner.

© **TIMES MEDIA PRIVATE LIMITED 2001**
Originated and designed by
Times Editions
An imprint of Times Media Private Limited
A member of the Times Publishing Group
Times Centre, 1 New Industrial Road
Singapore 536196
http://www.timesone.com.sg/te

PICTURE CREDITS
A.N.A. Press Agency: 33
Archive Photos: 12, 17
Bes Stock: 2, 20, 24, 45
Susanna Burton: 35
Focus Team: 29, 43
HBL Network: 3 (bottom), 13, 14, 15 (both),
    18, 23, 26, 30, 34, 37
Dave G. Houser: 3 (top), 7, 31 (both)
The Hutchison Library: 6, 19, 27
Earl and Nazima Kowall: 22 (bottom)
Photobank Photolibrary: 1, 3 (center), 9, 10,
    25, 28, 32, 39
David Simson: cover, 8, 21, 22 (top), 36, 40
Topham Picturepoint: 41
Vision Photo Agency: 11
Nik Wheeler: 4, 5, 16, 38

Digital Scanning by Superskill Graphics Pte Ltd

Library of Congress Cataloging-in-Publication Data
Yip, Dora.
Welcome to Cambodia / Dora Yip and Dayaneetha De Silva.
p. cm. — (Welcome to my country)
Includes bibliographical references and index.
ISBN 0-8368-2522-5 (lib. bdg.)
1. Cambodia—Juvenile literature. [1. Cambodia.]
I. De Silva, Dayaneetha. II. Title. III. Series.
DS554.3 .Y57   2001
959.6—dc21   2001017030

Printed in Malaysia

1 2 3 4 5 6 7 8 9 05 04 03 02 01

Contents

Words that appear in the glossary are printed in **boldface** type the first time they occur in the text.

4

Welcome to Cambodia!

Cambodia is a beautiful land. It was once a **flourishing** empire, but the country is now rebuilding after almost thirty years of war and destruction. Let's learn about Cambodia!

Opposite: Many Cambodians use bicycle rickshaws for transportation.

Below: The orange-yellow robes of Buddhist monks are a common sight in Cambodia.

The Flag of Cambodia

The Cambodian flag has two blue bands and one red band. Blue stands for royalty. Red represents the nation. The white symbol on the red band is the temple Angkor Wat. White represents Buddhism, Cambodia's main religion.

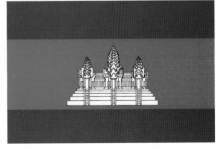

The Land

Cambodia has an area of 69,900 square miles (181,040 square kilometers). Thailand is northwest of Cambodia, Laos is to the north, and Vietnam is to the east. The Gulf of Thailand faces Cambodia's southwestern coast.

Most of Cambodia is a lowland area, but there are mountain ranges in the north and southwest. The northern Dangrek range forms a natural border

Below: Rice grows in wet fields called paddies. These paddies are near Kampong Chhnang.

with Thailand. The Cardamom range in the southwest contains Cambodia's highest peak, *Phnom Aoral* (puh-NAWM OW-ral), at 5,948 feet (1,813 meters).

The mighty Mekong River flows through Cambodia. Its **tributary**, the Tonle Sap, forms the largest inland lake in Southeast Asia. Annual flooding of these waters keeps the soil in the central plains rich and fertile. The central plains are Cambodia's most populated areas.

Above:
Some Cambodians make a living by catching fish in the Mekong River and the Tonle Sap.

Climate

Cambodia has a tropical climate that is always hot and humid. The average temperature is 80° Fahrenheit (27° Celsius). **Monsoons** create a wet season and a dry season. The wet season lasts from May through October. Mountain areas, especially the Cardamon Mountains, receive the most rain. The dry season lasts from November to May.

Below: Cambodia often has terrible floods during the wet season.

Left: The roots and branches of giant tropical trees are damaging and even destroying some of the ancient Khmer temples in Angkor.

Plants and Animals

Cambodia's vast forests are home to all kinds of wildlife, including tigers, clouded leopards, elephants, monkeys, and bears. A variety of freshwater fish and waterbirds live in and along the Mekong River and the Tonle Sap.

History

Historians believe that people have been living in Cambodia since about 4,000 B.C. The **Khmer** kingdom of Funan was the first great empire in Southeast Asia. It became part of the Chenla kingdom in the seventh century.

From Angkor to Indochina

The **golden age** of the Khmer empire began in A.D. 790 when a Khmer ruler named Jayavarman II took the throne.

Left: Rulers of the Angkor empire built fabulous temples and monuments. Although many of these buildings now lie in ruins, thousands of tourists visit them every year.

Left: Cambodia's King Norodom Sihanouk (*left*) met with French colonial secretary Coste-Flouret (*right*) during a visit to France in June 1948. Cambodia was part of French Indochina from 1884 to 1953. The French named Sihanouk king of Cambodia in 1941.

His **dynasty** ruled from the ninth century to the fifteenth century. Its kingdom was built around the city of Angkor. The Angkor empire fell apart after its last great ruler, Jayavarman VII, died. For the next five centuries, Cambodia was alternately controlled by Siam (Thailand) and Vietnam.

The country gained **stability** when it became part of the French colony of Indochina in 1884. France protected Cambodia from more invasions by Siam and Vietnam.

Independence and Civil War

In 1945, after World War II ended, France granted Cambodia **autonomy**. On November 9, 1953, King Norodom Sihanouk declared Cambodia's independence. Sihanouk left the throne in 1955 and became prime minister.

In 1970, however, General Lon Nol overthrew Sihanouk, and a civil war started. Sihanouk fled to China where he became an **ally** of the Cambodian

Below: During the civil war of the 1970s, Cambodians held a peaceful demonstration in the national stadium at *Phnom Penh* (puh-NAWM pen).

Left: Soldiers of the Khmer Rouge **persecuted** thousands of Cambodians, many of whom were educated people, such as teachers and monks. From 1975 to 1979, the Khmer Rouge killed about 1.5 million Cambodians.

communist leader, Pol Pot. When the government of Lon Nol collapsed in 1975, Pol Pot's Communist Party of Kampuchea took control of Cambodia.

The Khmer Rouge

Under Pol Pot's leadership, between 1975 and 1979, the *Khmer Rouge* (kuh-MAIR rooj), or the armed members of the communist party, turned Cambodia into a **labor camp**. An invasion by Vietnam in 1978 pushed the Khmer Rouge north toward Thailand, but its attacks on Cambodians continued.

Elections

Vietnam withdrew from Cambodia in 1989. Four years later, in 1993, Cambodia held national elections that named two prime ministers. Sihanouk's son, Prince Norodom Ranariddh, became first prime minister, and Hun Sen became second prime minister.

After another election in 1998, Hun Sen became the sole prime minister of Cambodia. That same year, Khmer Rouge leaders surrendered, finally giving Cambodians some hope for lasting peace.

Left: Buddhist monks were among the Cambodians who voted in the 1998 election.

Jayavarman VII
(c. 1120/25 – c. 1215/19)

Jayavarman VII ruled at the height of the Angkor empire. During his reign, art and architecture flourished.

Pol Pot (1928–1998)

Between 1975 and 1979, Pol Pot ruled Cambodia as a **dictator**. His government caused Cambodians great suffering. Pol Pot died mysteriously in 1998.

Pol Pot

King Norodom Sihanouk (1922–)

Norodom Sihanouk became Cambodia's king in 1941, at the age of eighteen. During most of the Khmer Rouge years, he lived under **house arrest** in Phnom Penh. Sihanouk was crowned king again in 1993.

King Norodom Sihanouk

Government and the Economy

Since 1993, Cambodia has been a multiparty democracy with a **constitutional monarch**. The king, who is the country's chief of state, chooses a prime minister, who is the head of government. The king also chooses the prime minister's **Cabinet**.

Below: A portrait of King Norodom Sihanouk hangs on the front of the Royal Palace in Phnom Penh. In Cambodia, a king rules for life. His successor is chosen by the Royal Council of the Throne but must be of royal blood.

Left:
Hun Sen has been
Cambodia's prime
minister since 1998.
Before becoming a
government official,
he was a member of
the Khmer Rouge.

The Branches of Government

The Cambodian government has three
divisions. The legislative branch has
an elected Assembly and an appointed
Senate. The executive branch includes
the prime minister, his Cabinet, and
a Council of Ministers. The judicial
branch is independent of the legislative
and executive branches. Its Supreme
Court and lower courts protect the
rights of Cambodian citizens.

Left:
Cambodia produces a lot of rubber. It is one of the country's leading exports. Cambodia's trading partners include the United States, Singapore, Japan, and Thailand.

Agriculture and Trade

Cambodia's main source of income is farming, especially growing rice. Its exports include timber, soybeans, rubber, and sesame. Its main imports are machinery and construction materials. In recent years, tourism has been an important industry, too.

Boosting the Economy

Cambodians are some of the poorest people in the world. More than 80 percent are farmers, who grow crops mostly to feed their own families. The Cambodian government is trying to boost the country's economy by educating its people, improving living conditions, and trying to attract aid from other countries.

Left: Fishing is an important source of income for Cambodians, especially for those living along the Mekong River and the Tonle Sap.

People and Lifestyle

More than 12 million people live in Cambodia. Most of them are in villages around the Mekong River and the Tonle Sap. Almost 90 percent of

Cambodians are Khmer. The modern Khmer is a mix of different cultural and **ethnic** groups, including Chinese, Vietnamese, and Cham. Most Khmer used to work as farmers, but many have now moved to the cities.

Above: When they are working outdoors, Khmer women and girls wear a *krama* (krah-mah), which is a large scarf that protects the head and neck from the hot sun.

A large number of Chinese also live in Cambodia. Before 1975, they were the largest minority group. Today, most of the Chinese are in Phnom Penh and other towns. Many of them are traders and bankers.

Below: The midday sun in Cambodia can be extremely hot, so these boys are staying inside to keep cool.

Among the Vietnamese living in Cambodia, some work in business, others fish for a living. Most Cham are fishermen or farmers. Their ancestors came from the Champa Kingdom, which once ruled most of Vietnam.

Family Life

Cambodian families are close-knit. Sometimes three generations live in the same household. Older parents often live with their children and help take care of their grandchildren.

At age three or four, Cambodian children start looking after themselves. By age ten, girls are expected to help their mothers with household chores, and boys help take care of the family's farm animals.

Above: When Cambodian children reach the age of five, they start to look after their younger brothers and sisters.

Cambodian Weddings

Although it is an old custom, parents and matchmakers still choose marriage partners for many young men and women in Cambodia.

In the past, Cambodian weddings lasted three days or more. Now, they usually last one day, but the ceremonies start very early in the morning, and the celebrations continue late into the night. The wedding ends with a banquet.

Above: Wedding ceremonies in Cambodia include rituals such as tying cotton threads soaked in holy water around the bride's and groom's wrists.

Opposite: In Cambodia, most houses in the countryside are built on stilts.

23

Education

The Cambodian education system was badly affected by civil war and Pol Pot's reign. Today, Cambodia still faces a shortage of schools, teachers, and educational materials.

Below:
In Cambodian classrooms, children sit at long wooden desks. Four or five children often share one textbook.

All public education is free in Cambodia. Most Cambodian children start school at the age of six or seven. Many of them, however, do not finish primary school, and few children go on to high school. Institutions for study beyond high school have only recently been established or reopened in Cambodia.

The Cambodian government is trying to educate children and adults throughout the country. An important

part of this education is passing on Khmer culture. Temple schools have been revived so children can learn the ancient Pali script and study Buddhist **scriptures**. Outside of school, children learn to be obedient and helpful.

Above: Only selected students may attend the School of Fine Arts in Phnom Penh. This special school trains young people in classical dance, music, and art.

Religion

Cambodians are free to practice any religion, but most are Theravada Buddhists. By living good lives and doing good deeds, Buddhists believe they will reach **nirvana**.

Good deeds include providing meals for monks or donating money, goods, and labor to the temples. Buddhist children often take care of trees and gardens at the temples.

Below: Buddhist monks lead simple lives dedicated to Buddhism and the temple. They are very disciplined and must follow more than 200 rules.

Left: These Cham Muslims have gathered outside a mosque after praying. For the Cham, Islam is a complete way of life. It is both their religion and their culture.

Other Religions

Islam is another important religion in Cambodia. It is practiced by the Cham, who are Sunni Muslims. A small number of Cambodians are Roman Catholic, Protestant, Taoist, or Confucianist. Whatever their religion, most Cambodians believe in supernatural spirits.

Language

Cambodia's official language is Khmer, but many adult Cambodians speak French or English. Khmer is a difficult language. It is based on the Indian classical languages, Pali and Sanskrit. Khmer has changed over time, however, and now contains Chinese, Thai, and French words. The Khmer "alphabet" has thirty-three consonants and twenty-three vowels.

Left: This sign is written in Khmer. Khmer is read from left to right, but the words often do not have spaces between them.

Left: This man is reading a Khmer newspaper outside a temple in Angkor.

Literature

Traditional Cambodian literature is based on the *Reamker*, which is a Khmer version of the Hindu epic, the *Ramayana*. Because many Cambodians cannot read or write, Khmer stories are told as folktales.

Since 1980, Cambodian writers have published several hundred works. Most of them are written in English and French, and almost all of them are about family tragedies that took place during the time of Pol Pot and the Khmer Rouge.

Arts

From beautiful handwoven silks to the detailed carvings that decorate wooden houses, art is part of everyday life in Cambodia. Cambodian art forms, such as sculpture and weaving, have been passed down from generation to generation. Most Khmer art has a religious theme, and the temple of Angkor Wat has become one of the world's artistic treasures.

Below: The roof of the Royal Palace in Phnom Penh is decorated with colorful tiles and elaborate designs.

Left: Cambodian temples hold many works of art. This tile panel is from the Wat Phnom temple in Phnom Penh.

Recovering Lost Culture

The Khmer Rouge **regime** destroyed all records of Cambodian culture and killed many musicians, dancers, and artists because they represented earlier rulers and dynasties. In the last ten years, foreign individuals and institutions have joined Khmers in efforts to restore traditional Cambodian art forms.

Below: *Apsaras* (ap-sah-rahs), or heavenly dancers, are very popular **motifs** in classical Khmer art.

Traditional Crafts

In Kampong Hluong, Cambodian silversmiths make beautiful bowls, plates, and candlesticks of imported silver. Women weave baskets out of jungle vines in villages west of Siemreab. Wood carvings show Cambodians' belief in the spirits of trees and flowers. Whenever a new house is built, a very small house is carved along with it. The small house is filled with food and flowers as an offering to the spirits.

Above: Skilled craftspeople made these unique Khmer pots. Cambodian craftwork also includes making jewelry and baskets.

Khmer Music

Traditional Cambodian music dates back to the Angkor empire. Khmer music is not written down. It is passed on from one musician to the next. Instruments used by Cambodian **ensembles** include cymbals, gongs, barrel drums, oboes, and xylophones. Modern Khmer bands, influenced by Western, Thai, and Chinese pop music, are trying new sounds.

Below: Cambodian artwork often shows scenes from the *Reamker.* This painting features Hanuman, the Hindu monkey god, and a mermaid queen.

Leisure

Cambodians are fun-loving people. Most cannot afford to go on vacations, but they take every opportunity to play with their children, get together with friends, and celebrate festivals.

Many Cambodian children do not have toys. They play with whatever they can find. Like most other children, they enjoy playing games, jumping rope, and running races.

Below:
Cambodians love to watch movies. In the 1960s, King Sihanouk himself made and starred in many movies.

Left: Cambodian children have very good imaginations. They can think up all kinds of ways to have fun playing in the water.

Urban households often have televisions, but Cambodian families and neighbors like to gather around one television set to watch the programs.

Shadow Puppet Theater

Shadow puppet theater is a cross between a movie and a play. It tells the stories of the *Reamker*, using as many as 150 puppets for one performance. Because shadow puppet theater was not allowed during the Khmer Rouge era, it is not performed very often anymore.

Sports

After years of war, the sports most Cambodians play are informal. Organized sports, such as soccer and basketball, however, are becoming popular again. Most organized sports events are held at the Olympic stadium in Phnom Penh.

Soccer

Soccer, which is called football, is popular throughout Cambodia. The Cambodian national team has competed in international matches, such as the World Cup Qualifiers.

Above: Young Cambodians enjoy playing soccer. Schools and universities organize league games between November and April.

Racing

Motorcross, or motorbike racing, has become popular in Cambodia in recent years. The annual dragon boat race, however, is the country's most colorful racing event. Rowers, dressed in team colors, compete in long, brightly painted boats.

Below: Dragon boats are lined up for the start of a race during the annual Water Festival. The festival is held in October or November.

Other Sports

Other popular sports in Cambodia include badminton, scuba diving, martial arts, and kickboxing. Many Cambodians believe that kickboxing actually started in their country.

Festivals

Cambodia's two largest festivals, the Khmer New Year and *Pisakh Bochea* (PEE-sahk BOH-CHEE-uh), are both held in April. Although the Khmer New Year is a religious festival, everyone dresses up in their best clothes and has a lot of fun. Pisakh Bochea **commemorates** the birth and **enlightenment** of the Buddha. Buddhists participate in religious processions and make offerings at the temples.

In July, Chol Vassa celebrates the beginning of both Buddhist Lent and the rainy season. Cambodians celebrate their country's independence from French rule on November 9.

Left: Parades and ceremonies highlight the opening of Cambodian temples, such as Wat Ku Tlok near Angkor.

Food

Cambodian cooking uses a lot of rice. The flavors of Thailand, Malaysia, and South Vietnam are present in many Cambodian dishes, but Chinese and French foods have had the greatest influence on Cambodian **cuisine**.

Cambodian Meals

Almost all Cambodian meals consist mainly of rice and soup. Common foods eaten with the rice include

Left:
Cambodians like to eat rice dumplings. They are available in many shapes, sizes, and flavors. They are even sold as snacks on streets throughout the country.

vegetables, fish, and fish products, such as *tuk trey* (tak trey), or fish sauce, and *prahok* (prah-hok), or fish paste. Meat and poultry are too expensive to be served very often.

Above: These young boys are eating their midday meal. At mealtime, all the food is set out at the same time, and people add a little bit of everything to their bowls of rice.

Cambodians love spicy food and strong flavors, so hot peppers, ginger, lemongrass, and mint are added to many Khmer dishes. Desserts usually are made only for special occasions.

Above: Many treasures from Angkor are kept at the National Museum in Phnom Penh.

Angkor B2

Banteay Mean Cheay
A1–A2
Batdambang A2

Cardamom
Mountains
A3–B3

Dangrek Mountains
A1–B1

Gulf of Thailand
A4–B5

Kampong Cham C3
Kampong Chhnang
(city) B3
Kampong Chhnang
(province) B2–B3
Kampong Hluong B3

Kampong Spoe
B3
Kampong Thum
B2–C2
Kampot B4
Kandal B3–C4
Kaoh Kong A3–B4
Keb B4
Krachen C2–D3

Laos C1–D1

Mekong River C1–C4
Mondol Kiri D2–D3

Otdar Mean Cheay
A1–B1

Phnom Aoral B3
Phnom Penh B3
Phnum Penh B3
Pouthisat A3–B2

Preah Seihanu
(Sihanoukville)
A4–B4
Preah Vihear B1–C2
Prey Veng C3–C4

Rotanah Kiri D1–D2

Siem Reab B1–B2
Siemreab B2
South China Sea
D4–C5

Stoeng Treng
D1–C2
Svay Rieng C3–C4

Takev B3–B4
Thailand A1–C1
Tonle Sap (lake) B2
Tonle Sap (river) B3

Vietnam D1–B5

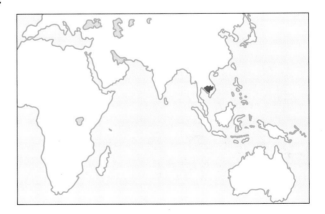

Quick Facts

Official Name	Kingdom of Cambodia
Capital	Phnom Penh
Official Language	Khmer
Population	12,212,306 (2000 estimate)
Land Area	69,900 square miles (181,040 square km)
Provinces	Banteay Mean Cheay, Batdambang, Kampong Cham, Kampong Chhnang, Kampong Spoe, Kampong Thum, Kampot, Kandal, Kaoh Kong, Krachen, Mondol Kiri, Otdar Mean Cheay, Pouthisat, Preah Vihear, Prey Veng, Rotanah Kiri, Siem Reab, Stoeng Treng, Svay Rieng, Takev
Municipalities	Keb, Phnum Penh, Preah Seihanu (Sihanoukville)
Official Religion	Theravada Buddhism
Highest Point	Phnom Aoral 5,948 feet (1,813 m)
Longest River	Mekong River
Largest Lake	Tonle Sap (Great Lake)
Currency	Cambodian riel (3,815 riels = U.S. $1 in 2000)

Opposite: The French built the Royal Palace in Phnom Penh in 1884.

44

Glossary

ally: a person, group, or nation that supports another in a special cause or purpose.

autonomy: self-government.

Cabinet: a special group of advisors selected to assist a country's head of government.

commemorates: remembers or calls to mind.

communist: related to a political system in which the government owns and controls all goods and resources.

constitutional monarch: a king or sovereign ruler of a nation that is governed according to the laws of an established constitution.

cuisine: a style of preparing and cooking food.

dictator: a ruler who has complete authority over a country.

dynasty: a family of rulers who inherit their power.

enlightenment: a state of intellectual or spiritual understanding.

ensembles: groups of musicians, actors, or dancers who perform together on a regular basis.

ethnic: related to a certain race or culture of people.

flourishing: growing and developing quickly; successful.

golden age: the most successful period in the history of a nation or people.

house arrest: holding a person under guard in his or her own home, instead of in a prison.

Khmer: the native people of Cambodia.

labor camp: a kind of prison where people are forced to do hard, physical work.

monsoons: strong, seasonal winds.

motifs: patterns or designs that follow a theme and are usually repeated.

nirvana: the highest level of spiritual enlightenment a person can achieve in the Buddhist religion.

persecuted: treated cruelly and unfairly for reasons related to politics, race, or religion.

regime: a system of government; the government currently in power.

scriptures: sacred or religious books or writings.

stability: firmness; steadiness; the strength to survive.

tributary: a river or stream that flows into a larger body of water.

More Books to Read

Angkat: The Cambodian Cinderella.
    Jewell Reinhart Coburn
    (Shen's Books)

Buddhist Temple. Places of Worship
    series. Angela Wood
    (Gareth Stevens)

Cambodia. Enchantment of the World
    series. Miriam Greenblatt
    (Children's Press)

The Clay Marble. Minfong Ho
    (Econo-Clad Books)

Judge Rabbit and the Tree Spirit: A
    Folktale from Cambodia. Cathy
    Spagnoli (Children's Press)

The People of Cambodia. Celebrating
    the Peoples and Civilizations of
    Southeast Asia series. Dolly
    Brittan (Powerkids Press)

A Visit to Cambodia. Visit to series.
    Rob Alcraft (Heinemann Library)

Videos

In the Shadow of Angkor Wat.
    (Home Vision Cinema)

Lost Spirits of Cambodia.
    (A & E Home Video)

Mysteries of Asia: Jewels in the Jungle.
    (Unapix)

Raising the Bamboo Curtain: Emerging
    Burma and Cambodia. (Questar)

Web Sites

sunsite.berkeley.edu/KidsClick!/
    midcoun.html

www.afk.com/resources/countryfacts/
    cambodia.tmpl

www.cybersleuth-kids.com/sleuth/
    Geography/Asia/Cambodia/

www.factmonster.com/ipka/
    A0107378.html

Due to the dynamic nature of the Internet, some web sites stay current longer than others. To find additional web sites, use a reliable search engine with one or more of the following keywords to help you locate information about Cambodia. Keywords: *Angkor, Cambodians, Khmer, Mekong River, Norodom Sihanouk, Phnom Penh.*

Index